W0114887

Selma Asotić

Say Fire

archipelago books

First published in BCSM as *Reci vatra* by *Buybook* and *Raštan izdavaštvo*, 2022
First Archipelago Books Edition, 2025

Library of Congress Cataloging-in-Publication Data available upon request.

ISBN 9781962770439

Archipelago Books
232 3rd Street #A111
Brooklyn, NY 11215
www.archipelagobooks.org

Cover art *Ruffled Feathers* by Ningiukulu Teevee
Interior designed and typeset by Gopa & Ted2, Inc.

The authorized representative in the EU for product safety and compliance is eucomply OÜ, Pärnu mnt 139b-14, 11317 Tallinn, Estonia, hello@eucompliancepartner.com, +33 757690241

This work is made possible by the New York State Council on the Arts with the support of the Office of the Governor and the New York State Legislature.

This publication was made possible with support from the Hawthornden Foundation, the Carl Lesnor Family Foundation, the Cornelia Bessie Memorial Foundation, and the New York City Department of Cultural Affairs.

PRINTED IN CANADA

Contents

SAY FIRE

Landscape with footprints in ash

You must leave for the story to begin
is what fairytales taught me.
I left. My ghosts
now trail behind and weep. I try to comfort them.
At night I place a bowl of milk
on the terrace. I promise
a trip to the sea. They disappear.
When I'm alone in the room
all catastrophes are easily traceable.
I bury my mind. Useless mill
churning voices, plastic straws, bills,
hands demanding to give
and give and give.
My own hands I fling
down the river. At the estuary
they remember everything.
In my head
is a circle farm. If I die, this very moment,
no one will finish what I set out
to say. What will you do then,
my misery? Already August. In heat,
things expand. So do minutes.
Fire swallows trees, entire forests.
At some point, there won't be anything
left to burn. Fire
has no future. What a relief
for the fire.

No one writes home

Words sleep in the warm
burrow of our breath.
We wave goodbye.
Next comes distance.
Old fears we once whispered
to the walls for when the saints
come marching.
I try on hand-me-down cities,
oversized and worn through by the solitude of others.
Monuments go by. Fields
deep in thought. Plazas go by and with them
chatterbox fountains. On a clothesline
shirts flutter like surrender. I stare
into a thousand nights and at the bottom of some
is a face that loves me. The sky stays the same,
darling and handsome. A continent
lullabies itself into water.
I imagine you on the other side,
in the same room where I tried to read
your waverings in the ictus of smoke.
Mother, what comes next
          are the saints who never come.
No divine secret left
to find, nothing to the world
but arms, like lighthouses,
tireless in searching.
Hear me speak then,
with the hunger of those born
to lose, my voice
          wide as daybreak.

First time in the only lesbian bar in my town

Holy black hole in the wall   tonight I wear my best
   despair and a skin-sack of bones three jinns
have earthquaked to rubble.
                 Like light I've come
                        to never leave.
In bathroom stalls the girls rise
  like hallelujah pressed against the doors.
I want what I want, I declare—
         here omniscient mouths can sing
                  a body into the future.
    I'm just waiting to be touched
exactly where I want to disappear and if a hand
            should reach for the small of my back it might find
everything already forgiven.   Don't say desire.
I'm looking for a palm to unsun myself on
     and I know you've seen stars
             die before but never quite
    this keenly, my dark
        soot-crying vault,
            take me as I am, prairied
      and as of yet whole,   fearless
               shaking a little.

Coming out

In the house there was a body next to
another body and in each body
a throat and in each throat
a bone. I saw her move
through a crowd nonchalant
like fire. Entire skies
hungered on my skin.
        I'm trying to explain.
Sometimes you need to lie to tell
the truth is what poetry taught me.
I'll say:
there was once a city and in the city
an earthquake and in the earthquake
laughter lines. I reached
for my pocket and found
lint and keys and a brood of planets
and someone's discarded rivers.
The furrow of dawn. Loving
that comes never like the night
because it has no such patience.
        I'll start over.
A body—one,
then the other. Fingers tumbling
down the skin like September.
Afterwards, a room
gorged on light. Afterwards, you turn
in the doorway mother and ask
if I'm one of them.
Words, poetry taught me,
are like teeth—they are what they are.

Miniscule knives.
In each knife a heart
that throbs
and throbs.

A lover learns my tongue

No open field or house
made of windows. In this language you kneel,
you scrape with your voice tar
from the walls until it silts
the roof of your mouth.

The way the sun enters
through the curtains, pawing
the unknown face on the bed,
you too enter on tiptoe—
        against you everything
that won't let me go,
against you armies and sirens bleating red,
why is every language a funeral?
Above our bodies pulped to dark
mustachioed verbs collapse
their batons.
        Lay down
your arms. Pretend dead.
When they come closer kiss me
        with all of god's holy names.

Monologue for a first date

Like a matchstick I contain infinite
promise, my head ablaze, a dent
in the night. Skilled in cloud-conduct, lazing over
cities strewn with gutted years. The industrious
hate the look of me, emergencies tug at my sleeve
while I preoccupy myself with time
stretching in a jar of honey.

Some revolutions flirted then dropped me
a *seen*. Overly sensitive, lover
of incurable endings, I never forget mouths
that precioused my name. Unafraid,
except at night. If upon waking I see light
singed to white noise, I turn to my grief and ask
how long. I watch her take off her shoes.

Offspring of indreaming, deformed
reverist, for no special occasion
I treat my body to an entry wound
in which to collapse. Cursed with a heart
pumping dactyls. My business is breathing
to devour myself.

Aubade with a 104° fever

All catastrophes know us
by name and address,
someone's buried in our breaths
the certainty of bad news.

Within you, generations
of betrayed smiles now rise in riot—

we never learned a thing.

On a scream's empty parcel we set up
an amusement park,
munched on corncobs while in the hills
autumns multiplied.

I'm already forgetting you
with all of my skin.
I'm forgetting you with all the roads you are yet
to take, in the wind I build
a cathedral of your voice.

Someday,
someone will stand before you, and you'll
realize
time is just a trick by which the sun renews
its vow to the flowers.

All we need to do is withstand
this morning, as it waves at us with hands
that know how to hold something beautiful
without bitterness.

My father's skin looks like the surface of the moon

They told you shrapnel made men
celestial, that's why you joined
the army. In midsummer, when weathervanes
carousel, you pull your silence
taut over our house. Nothing bad
will happen to us now, not with you
standing sentinel at the edge
of our sleep, guarding
against the peacethieves.

In the living room you and I mummify
waiting for the rains to pass.
Dust settles on our eyelids, the choleric
mahogany. Should you ever speak, I'd tie
my hair to the hooves of your voice,
I'd have my death by dragging
out what the water dreams sunk. I'd ask
if you've seen the moles
in the garden, the bird nest
under the eaves. I'd ask how many
you captured. How many did you kill?

Uncle

I imagine three hooks in the hallway. On the first a winter hat, on the second a coat, and on the third, a pineapple grenade hanging by the trigger. I imagine his broad shoulders and the grey hair at the back of his head as he approaches and takes first the coat, then the grenade, then the hat. As he turns to face the door on the left I see his profile, the stutter of capillaries under his ear.

That's not how it happened.

No one writes home

Write me when you can.
Skip the hellos. There's time left only

for the unbearable. Instead of settled,
let me say lost. Instead of scenic, let me say,

on this continent cities are orchestras
of hammers out of sync. Some Sundays

find a way to be kind. In their cranked-up light
passersby grow intimate on sidewalks

suddenly brave they ask:
when it comes for us, the great

big quiet, will it be gossamer at first,
then, obsidian?

Write me when you can.
Skip the weather reports. In this very moment

someone is weeping, someone
somewhere is inconsolable,

and all we do is wait for our turn.
How awful we were. Speaking,

as if to speak was to yawn
in the glow of a warm afternoon,

the dust still trembling with the laughter
of dinner guests. All our end-stopped questions.

       Instead of comfort
let me say fire.

Instead of forgive
let me say fire. Instead of October

let me say light is the color of a bullet. Look
at the air, mother. The air is full of it.

Sarajevo–New York, 2019

Self-portrait drawn as a circle

A parrot's heart is the size of a seed.
When machine guns croak, the first to burst
will be the heart of the parrot, followed by the glass jar in Mother's head.
        That's how it begins.
With a bullet hole in the door for Nana to peek through
and come back with the report: *Not yet.*
        We pray louder.
And louder the trees fall. Aunt's stockings
are torn and red as she crawls through the city,
a sniper's eye longing to inscribe on her chest
its frivolous will, until
she gets up and vertical
runs into the fifth of her seven lives.
        That's how it begins.
And lasts. All around us
spring dreams out loud. Nana hurls
a throatful of syllables at the wind and the pattern reveals—
her daughter on the balcony, serious,
like the sea depths, explaining the theory of gravity to the clothespins.
It's clear now that no solitude will spare us.
        That's how it begins.
With the sky as pure forgetting.
God doesn't exist, but in any case, we pray louder.
Only Azrael is always there. With Nana he sits
by the bed of neighbor Raza in whose spleen
a foreign army is sending forth its blackshirts.
Is it time, Nana asks. It's time.
Raza's eyes open and in them Nana sees:
        —we will die in empty rooms,
the life that could've been passing through us

like a final insult.
On the frontlines, her sons dream of black
wrecking balls, the rustling of paper behind closed doors.
They return inconsolable. She has nowhere
to return because no place is more dangerous
than the one she comes from—the intuition
of a woman. That's how it begins.
With mother's exhausted milk. Feeding me,
Aunt says, very close: *Little one,*
death is no aunt for you to trust it so blindly.
She doesn't know it yet, but she's stepped
into the seventh of her seven lives.
   Here come the men,
back from the war. Some
more despised than others.
I can't remember,
Mother says, *where we buried him.*
He couldn't have been bigger than a palm,
would've fit into a pack of cigarettes, tiny
he was and smooth
like a marble.
   That's how
every history begins. Something bursts,
and everyone clutches their chests to see
if it is they who burst. A parrot's heart
is the size of a seed. In a cigarette pack,
entangled in oak roots, it swells again. Naïve
like a circle. Remembering nothing.

My father and I, seven fathoms later

Bedtime and we retreat
each into our own regret. I think of the sea.
The two of us walking between the cliffs
and the bougainvillea. I was testing
how close I could get to the edge before
the leash of your arm pulled me back.
You were explaining seagulls
and how ships remained afloat despite
their great weight. That's when I learned
the advantage of being hollow.
We stopped at a fruit stand.
The girl was pulling her hair into a bun.
Reaching over the crates, she picked
for us grapes and figs, plums, one of which
harboured a worm. While she worked
the scales, I followed with my eyes
the line of sweat from the collarbone to a hidden
ripening under her tank top.
On our way back, you hummed a tune.
The plastic bags swayed,
cutting into my palms
summer's end. The sweetness. The heft of it.

There's a coat hanger in the hall. He unhooks his jacket, swings it around and puts both arms through at once. He does this slowly. Then he bends over and puts on his boots, first the right, then the left. All the while, he's whistling. He moves to unlock the door and holds it ajar as he shouts to his wife, who is somewhere in the house, always busy, *Baha, I won't be long.*

He walks across the courtyard to the workshop. The wooden door opens to a confusion of metal and sawdust. He kicks a foam block out of his way and in three languid strides approaches the shelf on the back wall. (One must imagine now, also, the smell of syntelan in his nostrils, behind him specks of dust whirpooling in a sunbeam, November maturing in corners.) He reaches behind one of the toolboxes and lets his fingers read the chill of ribbed iron, then grip the solid body. On his palm, it looks like a sleeping sparrow.

That's not how it happened.

Ode to my nation

Everything that does not love me
is you, invigilator, blister
on my soul, my sleepless flight,
fight me or uproot
from my blood, you neverending
graveyard of clocks,
every sun in you dripping rust
into my irises, lip-hasp, lullabied sear,
welcome me with a crucifix
that is my citizenship, welcome me with life
whittled down to a whistle, whistle me
like a pretty tune in the dark for no one
to hear, hurt me loveless, snarl
of my nightmare, nightshade pressed
between the ribs,
come at me my debt my un-
forgivable, come
let me tell you something.

Theodicy

after Matija Gubec

God is great, you exclaim, forehead
on the floor. Outside, a halo of moonlight
rusts discarded next to the road
where the soldiers passed, their boots
like thunderclaps hammering the earth
into a sheet of copper. God is great, you say,
then three times wash your arms. Meanwhile,
the trees are all gone. There's only a forest
of phantom limbs, only a spluttering
fire under your roof, only you
still murmuring even in sleep
inna nahnu nuhyil mawta. God is great,
you exhale, as your granddaughter traces
the growth rings on your skin, and decides
she doesn't know what to do
with this house built on a landslide
of your hope, this faith useless to the living.
Hard of prayer, she finally understands
God is great, if you're kneeling.

He's a blue-eyed boy whistling on his way home from school. The oak trees lining the cobbled square know him intimately. In the general store Čika Mišo encourages him to grab a handful of candies from the glass bowl on the counter. He's too excited and too young to notice his mother's relief when Mišo looks her in the eyes and says it's on the house. His mother's winter coat smells of jasmine, of frayed upholstery in provincial theater houses where she feeds lines to faltering actors drunk on šljivovica, of Cyrano de Bergerac read too many times. Fifty-five years later, in 2017, he'll stand in the doorway, looking at his mother lying on the couch in the room where he once carved his name into the drawer with a penknife. He'll try to take in her face, commit to memory its pruned tenderness. He'll say *you better start on that coffee, I'll swing by later.* That's not how it happened.

He's a blue-eyed boy shrieking like a piglet in a slaughter house, the barber having arrived to circumcise him years later than is customary. He cries his sisters out of the house and into the shed where they crouch behind the wheelbarrow, covering their ears. Amidst the humming of what they think is their blood, a voice they will later call consciousness says *you will remember this forever,* a verdict that severs them from their childhoods.

Later that year, he walks back home from the schoolyard carrying a ball under his right arm. A flock of birds is circling the minaret of the nearby mosque. Always, whenever he looks, the birds are there, circling the slender tower, as if some master builder had planned them together with the stone. He's blissfully tired and covered in sweat, kicking a pebble down the desolate street. Maybe it's the heaviness of late fall pressing down on the houses crooked and serried like the teeth in his mouth. Maybe it's the day the color of wet cement, or the oaks beckoning him to hurry home because his mother and sisters are now sitting down for supper, but he suddenly feels a vague urgency rising in his stomach. Overwhelmed, he stops. He looks up through the crosshairs of branches and says it for the first and only time: *please give me back my father*. That evening, when the twilight has solidified into clumps of coal, his mother asks *what took you so long*. She looks at him defenseless, knowing that he's festering into a man of few words.

That's not how it happened.

Unreliable witness

We were happy.
      We had a garden.
Even when they relocated
the city into past
tense, we found among the rocks
dandelions, drops of honeysuckle.
We weren't afraid of death. Only of how much
we'd miss each other. That morning,
he went out in his yellow sweater,
at the door he said *my dear*
        [   ]
memory is dirt under the fingernails.
The night was full of flames. Fireflies.
Those are fireflies floating in the moon's
bleary eye, I said, and walked.
And walked. My shadow telling time, in the dirt,
on the page where pinned lies
our every shudder, let there also be this:
      in the distance, the horizon tightened its lips.
The air carrying woodpecker
telegrams is all I remember, your Honor,
while your gavel proclaims:
The witness has been warned.
None of this is relevant to the proceedings.

Becoming a homeland

In the beginning, you are land—
a pause between a place to leave
and a place to get to.
From a window someone tosses out
a forest of palms. Daylight winces.
Someone is now clearing vistas,
inside you are houses, erect
interruptions step out to exchange
barley and fat, cut down the linden tree and carve
nightingales from its wood because
nightingales are pretty. No other reason.
How silly. You also find them pretty.
Someone then shouts *mine*,
sets a suspicion rolling down the road.
Logs in the forest bristle with moss.
Terror in calyces. Door at the wolf.
Palms whet the wind into winter,
unripen to fists. Everything you touch
starts to growl.

History

I'm the face above your face
observing you darkly,
orphaned by the cold dawn of December.

Do you remember nothing from your life?
The paper triple-folded
in your backpack, unloosening
a tie. And how you moved through doorways
terminally disaffected, on occasion paralyzed
by the usual questions.

Listen: flags
summersault under your window.
A spent voice is singing
Lili Marlene.

Do you remember
nothing from your life?
Do you not recognize this face
above your face, observing you darkly?
The alarm clock
shudders awake. Outside the armies
are already marching, and you, half-asleep,
follow their beat.

No one writes home

These days a thorn bush
hums in my throat and I tend to it
with seawater. No other news.
The landscape is still the same
tired thing: paper
pressed flat, and a crumpled pulse.
Sometimes,
      I go down to the coast to watch a wave
retract its gesture. How we consume
ourselves. How the wave
erases nothing but its own longing.

Once, I wanted to return,
but already a sky lay withered
in the window, so I set off
to where the body is a net
lowered into the wind.
If I ever arrive, if I ever
forget, maybe the world
will become a surge of oleander,
and I a floating thing.

      With love,

Enraged, he makes a dash across the training ground, splashing mud on the conscripts and the drill instructors. Someone yells *Waddaya think you're doing*, but he's already tackling the bastard. It takes five pairs of arms to wrench him away. *I didn't know she was your sister, swear to God*. He's still shaking when brought before the sergeant, only this time he shakes with fear, and not of the sergeant, but of his sister, of what she'll write in her letter when she finds out. He spends the rest of the military service avoiding his former friend. They reconcile when he becomes his brother-in-law.

Winter of 1992 has the metallic blue sheen of a grudge. It's Tuesday. On the other side of the mountain hulking above the city his brother-in-law crawls across the forest floor while enemy snipers take turns going for a clean-shot kill, straight through the head. A few miles away, he's being appointed commander of a small unit. He steps out of the makeshift barracks. From his vantage point he sees the entire city. Somewhere in it, his sister is hurtling down the staircase of a tower block with a two-month-old in her arms, the last one to leave, but she doesn't even make it past the first flight of stairs. They're trudging up in the opposite direction, fully armed and reeking of vodka. Six of them. One gets overly excited and shoots a round of bullets that flies right above her head. Before she can remind herself to keep quiet, her voice steps forward and bellows something like *Easy being an armed dickhead in front of a newborn*. They watch her, amused. One of them, the commander, looks down at her bare feet and flexes his jaw. He orders her back into the apartment. Retreating, she hears him say to the soldiers *Nobody gets into that flat but me*.

Standing in front of the barracks he scans the cluster of rooftops at the foot of the mountain. He's looking for a flock of birds circling a minaret. Once his finds it, he pulleys his gaze down an imaginary rope and locates the building of the elementary school. In one of the houses close to the school, his mother is now throwing hardcover books into the furnace.

She hears the pleading floorboards, the sound of jewelry grabbed by the handful, drunken shouting. She's crouching under the kitchen island, pressing the child into her body, willing her not to cry. The noise ebbs for a moment, then surges again, stars crashing in a rattle shaken by some bawling demiurge, the clatter of knives around the soldiers' belts setting a beat to the chattering of her bones. Her flesh is a plucked string, bared alertness following the sound of heavy boots running down the stairs, expecting any second the sound of the door busted open, everything suspended, everything enveloped by a time-lessness that pestles her into a mesh of horrible premonitions, every-thing sharpened to a high-pitched clarity that assaults her senses at once and doesn't abate until the quiet that's been trickling toward her finally pools in her skull. She opens her eyes. Through the kitchen window she sees the mountain. A ray of sunlight illuminates a square on the floor. Whirlpools of dust. She's alone in the building.

They all survive the war. His mother, his sisters, his brother-in-law. The Americans broker a peace agreement and bring in a constitution nobody voted for, written in a language no one speaks. In the summer of 1996, he walks down a dirt road to the army headquarters, pleased that nothing overly tragic has happened. He hands over the rifle, but doesn't return the two hand grenades in his backpack. The right corner of his mouth arches up, crumpling his face into a permanent snarl. He feels a little like God, and no one would disagree. A mean motherfucker, he leaves the army barracks whistling.

Decades later, the local newspapers will break the news: ANOTHER WAR VETERAN BLOWS HIMSELF UP. PEACETIME CLAIMS ANOTHER VICTIM. WAR VETERAN, BELOVED FAMILY MAN, KILLS HIMSELF, NO NOTE FOUND. OPPOSITION LEADERS CLAIM: THE STATE HAS LET OUR HEROES DOWN. My brother on the phone, screaming at a journalist: *At least use his initials, his mother doesn't know yet.*

That's not how it happened.

Monologue for a second date

Mostly, I stare at the ceiling and think
about how much I don't want to die. I have a head.
In my head is a circle farm. A woman waves
from a burning roof. There's also falling
from sixth-floor balconies, windshields,
suicide bombers, stairs, my eyeballs smeared
against the windshield, safety pins, shawls
caught in car wheels, knots, snowdrops.
I have a head. In my head is a stomach
full of butterflies. The butterflies are often sharks
and they want out. I let them out.
They trip on the threshold and smash their teeth.
I have a head. Inside is a living room. A suicide bomber's
watching syndicated comedy. My head plays
only reruns, cleaner ads, wet floors,
skulls cracked open. Nothing after that. All dark, all
air chastising its emptiness into the thought of you.
I squeeze my eyeballs shut
and think of you. I think of you
in as many ways as the rains falls.

Lessons from a war

it never ends.
after the cleric, thief, and chief commander comes
the intellectual. not necessarily in that order.
in hotel rooms, years later, you dream
of a face behind closed doors, the tip of a gun at your nape,
destiny perhaps postponed yet relentless
like the eyes of marina tsvetaeva. every time is the first time.
because the body remembers, but learns nothing.
       it never ends. some other names
are now bleeding on CNN's chyron, instead of your burning house
the screen shows a man giving his child
to a soldier. his hands are the hands of your father,
or the father of your father, same difference.
you are somewhere, among the blessed, on some square
you sip an espresso, the woman next to you says
how awful. your contempt blooms precious and pure.
       it never ends. war follows you through continents
in ragged caravans. every war is your war. when at the border crossing
an american cop asks *where are you from* you point
to everywhere that is disappearing. at the supermarket,
among the eggplants, blueberries from peru in december,
your rabbit heart flees from the realization that we're all
going to die. at the cash register you hear *fivefiftyplease*
and you remember
the chocolate bars in the fist of an UNPROFOR peacekeeper,
the cards with pretty blond boys he says are called backstreet.
this is when it began, your precious
pure contempt of anyone with something to give.
       it never ends. the running.
behind you, war drags his old bones. he reads

an op-ed by a concerned intellectual: *we must stop the balkanization*
   of america.
you laugh, so sweetly, you and your war.
from your mouth spills an ore
of suspect origin. in passing
you speak to the ironed shirts: do you know
of the circling of bones in nature? man is first
skin and bone, then just bone in broad daylight, bone
in the ground, it turns up in your garden with the may floods,
you pick it up to stir the tea because your war
has developed a nasty cough.
on thanksgiving, fireworks go off and you hide
under the table. because the body remembers
but learns nothing. it's hard
convincing your own body it has survived.
         it never ends. after the cleric, thief, and chief
commander comes the investor. your contempt
blooms precious and pure. a new yorker
staff writer tweets: *compassion is not the first thing that comes to mind*
when one thinks of the balkans.
you laugh, so sweetly, you and your war.
then you must take him to the bathroom,
you hold his head while he pukes, you comfort him
it's alright, my old man,
i still remember you.
you sit by him on the cold tiles.
because there's nothing
left to do, and there's no one else here,
except you and your war.

they descend upon us

the American PhDs, eager to investigate *this part of the world so often plagued by bursts of inter-ethnic violence.* Before they arrived we never knew murder was indigenous to our hands, a thing that blooms at regular intervals like the laughter of history. Nick from Connecticut is here to inspect. A peace studies graduate, whenever there's war Nick from Connecticut is deployed to spread common sense, ask the right questions—why, instead of why not. The more we war the more we need Nick from Connecticut, a few more genocides and he'll join the tenure track. O Nick from Connecticut! We'll come through for you, pocket twenty dollars for our *informed consent.* We'll be your very own *local informants.* Conveniently anonymous. Ready to talk on cue. So we do, and O Nick from Connecticut, yours is the outrage of all folks whose countries would never ever. Yours is a tender soul, there goes compassion dripping from your face onto the floor. It snakes across the room and up our legs. It leaves a trace of hot slime burning through our skin. How do we scrub off your *sorry so sorry?* No matter what we say you and your wheat-colored hair will never know how fast the shadows lengthen when you try to outrun them. You too are someone's sweet baby boy, your name Garamond-friendly, your mother on the phone to Aunt Linda *I'm so glad he gets to have this experience.* O Nick from Connecticut! It's your mother's marble kitchen top we covet, the bobbing blond lock, the gentle ignorance of the butcher's blade. What could it know of the things it severs? In the acknowledgments you'll express *sincere gratitude to survivors whose stories testify to the need for restorative justice and transversal reconciliation in the subliminal space of post-conflict contexts.* After you we lie wide-eyed for a long time, trying to remember our names. Drool trickles down our chins. Because we're imagining tying you to a chair, bashing in your head, sweet, little Nick from Connecticut.

Questions my mother will never ask

Is it cold where you live? Is it crowded?
Is it true what they say about the river there,
that it's not fickle like the rivers
we've known? I spend my days
watching the news, wondering, isn't it time
I had something to do with explosions?
Do you remember the New Year
when fireworks went off and we
ducked under the table? Is it true
what they say about dogs
being afraid of fireworks? Are we like dogs,
in that respect? Do you remember the cold
fire of the furnace? In spring,
our shame before the begonias?
Is it true what they say about the river there, that it's not
vengeful or scabrous like the rivers we've known?
Is the city where you live a big one? Is it large enough
to get lost? Are you lost—
the last time I looked into your face,
where was I supposed to find you? Who are you in the eyes
of the bus driver watching you punch
the ticket? Or the woman
smiling from across the bar? Do you smile back?
My daughter, who has travelled farther
than I can imagine, do you feel, sometimes,
when walking down the street, someone else walking behind you?
Do you turn? Do you remember
I cut the shape of you out of stray
desire? Why then
should we ever be afraid? Are you coming back?
If yes, do you know how to pack

a breath deep enough to outlast
the drowning? Because the rivers here
are single-minded, bottomless,
and have you ever seen anyone escape.

He was a blue-eyed boy whistling on his way home from school. The oak trees lining the cobbled square knew him intimately. Now he passes them one last time, but doesn't look up. Once in the narrow street, he reminds himself to pick a spot where the explosion is least likely to damage the neighbors' houses. The widest berth of space is where the street bends into a U-shape before continuing in a straight line to the elementary school. That's where he stops, right in the middle. One must now imagine birds circling a minaret, an open window on one of the houses, the sound of the newsman's voice simmering in the radio, the smell of stewed bell peppers and coriander. He takes his hands out of his pockets, uncoils his right fist. The grenade lies like a fallen sparrow on his palm. One last inscrutable thought scurries across his mind. He pulls out the pin.

Somewhere in the city, a phone rings.
My mother collapses to the floor.

Trolley bus blues

Our joint exhaustion sways the bus
in the rhythm of a limping surf.

We look at each other as if to attest, yes
you're still here, and isn't it sad

having to die when we're so
full of questions, still warm, right here,

our hands touching on the rail.
We wait for the doors to open.

Every one of our steps will enroot
a new future of nothing in particular.

We pass the man on the corner still
peddling hot chestnuts, and the longer

we stare at something as simple as the sky
the more incredulous we become.

How did we get here? Among trees
whose branches might need us, for without

our prone bodies they'd have one less
purpose in the world. Just a little longer, please.

One more walk down the block,
past cars with engines idling.

One more winded ascent,
the turning of the key.

One more *I'm home!* addressed
to someone who won't reply.

My aunt smokes and thinks of nothing

As she inhales, a fire runs chase round
the cigarette's rim, its revolution
ending in ash. She remembers it well.
Of ash she dreamt when for three nights and three
years the war blazed and the fevered city
vomited carcasses of cars, smashed glass
she sidestepped fleeing in her high heels,
wondering what they'd say to her mother—
your daughter, ma'am, was dressed to kill—
until down came the ash, softly falling
over the braille of broken psalms and now
she exhales. June in her garden, delayed
in bloom. The lilies grow. Zinnias too.
Love-in-a-mist. The cancer in her womb.

Nana

In my dream she enters
her own house through
a broken window, on her back,

a wildfire. She sets it down
next to her dowry
of clenched teeth

and a premonition.
Her husband
is a learned man, but when

at twenty the spindle
leaves her womb
riddled

with heartbeats,
she knows
more than he will ever know.

The wildfire burns,
each flame a deep-set
streak across her forehead.

In my dream
she enters her own house
through a broken window,

on her back, treason.
Ramadan,
and no salt for the broth.

She voids
her tear ducts into a pot,
hears learned voices in the walls

whisper to her of the Iblis
that is the woman. The bracts
along her spine pout with seeds

of heat. Deep within her
is a knowledge
ready to immolate.

In my dream she enters her own house
through a broken window,
on her back, the one hundredth

name of God. In my dream she looks
at me. Looks at me a long time,
her forehead

a bed of ploughed ash.
She strikes
from her eyes a dowry

of embers. Looks at me.
I call her haqq.
I call her nur.

Matrilineage

One is mayhemed
into threads, another weaves
a mesh, a third collects.

One tallies years
on her wrists, another
bends the bars, a third exits.

One tucks a thorn
under her tongue, another
grows a throat, a third insists.

One bites the fist
that gags her mouth, another
swallows teeth. A third hawks.
Speaks.

Grandmother ascends to heaven

1.

When I look at light
   pinned to the floor

the afternoon seems
   impossibly long.

     A shadow's
tremor, and it's gone.

I'm left with a shard
   of forgotten thought,

stacked nightfalls
   in the cupboard, yellowing.

2.

Bent into a silent
   question mark I crochet
dark's coattails.

     On TV, history
   is gatecrashing one city
or another.

     The glare of the moon
as it tries to place me,

     someone familiar
who dropped her face
at the threshold,

     counterfeit blood.

The man asleep
        on my bed mutters
names,

        names sweet
        as promise

a call
wreathing around my ankles,
            insisting.

3.

Nothing left,
but to get here.

My arms subterraned,
    as rivers do when they discover
the horizon spent.

A shadow's tremor, then
                —time

like precious china,
        never touched by weeping riddles.

I find them, so many
        honey-cured and unafraid,

their unbraided throats
        drying on the shore.

What succeeds
        eternity for now
isn't a concern.

Elevated
from the lawlessness of hands,
        we gather our strength.

God awaits
   in the thicket, snoring
through centuries.

God is still here,
   but you already knew that.

Assimilation

The barista waits for me to recall
the name of the drink I order every
morning. I'm sorry, I say, the word
invades me. His look
is a sealed envelope. Here, the river
overthinks itself into a sheet of ice. Faces slide.
The upturned collars. Mansard roofs and the stench
of mulch. I stop to inspect the cups
on sagging stalks. Grandmother once told me
what they were called, the pop of syllables
still going off somewhere in my mind.
If only I wasn't so unburdened.
Emptied of explosions. There,
there now, no one says. Into the soil
I cry a burst watermain. I stare
At the leaves. Waiting, as they wait
to receive the news of their survival.

Home as a list of superstitions

*

if opened inside the house, umbrellas foreshadow death

In our version of love, whoever is spared
stops at no sea. That year, swallows
departed with roof tiles in tow.
All winter long our house
was a well, and we mistook
sinking for sleep.
We told each other: it is better
to die in the wilderness, alien
to what loved you, better to die
among beasts who are nobody's witness.
All winter long we kept
our ears above water, catching
the echoes of cadavers as they hit the ground.
When the walls gave in, my arms
mistook heads for flotsam,
pushing them under on my way out.

*

if caught outside at dusk, you will be taken by jinns

When the day bruises
into the knowledge of roots,
we find ourselves outside free
of skin. A jinn pulls
a pit over our heads.
In constellations of weed bulbs
we read: here lie those
who waited for life to happen.
When I start to claw, you'll stuff

your ears with bits of dirt, so as not to hear
the laughter of the living.
Because our love has always
been like this: a turning of the head when at night
someone tiptoes out the door.

*

who stands still for too long must suffer the cobwebbed sky

Among you I was buried
in warmth. Now I live
as a wayward storm,
thoroughly balkanized, balking
at this country—America,
with her armless strangulations,
her sequoias sprouting
from vanquished mouths.
Surrender, I hear her say,
you won't change the names
given to history: your
senseless homicides, my reluctant duty.
All we ever did was forget
only light can trespass the edge
and remain whole. I straddled
each rift, spurred it into December.

*

once on your way it is bad luck to return

In our version of love, we saw
each other open, we each plant
in the other's chest a signpost.
It was a long time ago.
Now I have before me a path
bright with absence, and I walk it with my head

screwed on backwards. The wind scolds
the space between my feet—
                no one who remembers this
will call it escape.
Here is my road, mother,
threaded through unfurnished
days. I don't need
any directions. I need you
to look at my arms and tell me
they are blameless.

No one writes home

Something is always breaking
in the sky above us. I'm trying to recall
your hands cupping fireflies.
       Late August.
On our skin summer
wouldn't quit. I stumbled
catching up with you already disappeared
beyond the lip of the hill, the dead mouths
of soldiers below whispering
the secret of roots to the poppies.

I ran after you, through thistle-rayed
sunlight, believing the river when it swapped
our reflections with a shrug.

       I've learned now,
          once a cloud breaks the blue
rushes in to salvage the split.
The sky is merely a rumor of lost things.

Everywhere I look, your shadow
is still vanishing over the horizon.
       And I'm still
running towards you, with outstretched arms.
I'm running
back to you mother,
all the time.

archipelago books
is a non-profit publisher devoted to
promoting cross-cultural exchange through innovative
classic and contemporary international literature
archipelagobooks.org

elsewhere editions
translates luminous picture books from around the world
elsewhereeditions.org